"Azure Cloud Infrastructure:

Understanding the Basics"

BY

Issa Ngoie

CONTENTS

1. **Introduction to Azure Cloud Infrastructure**

- Explanation of what Azure Cloud Infrastructure is and how it works
- Overview of the different components of Azure Cloud Infrastructure, such as virtual machines, storage accounts, and networks
- Explanation of the benefits of using Azure Cloud Infrastructure, such as scalability and flexibility

2. **Setting up an Azure Cloud Infrastructure**

- Explanation of how to create an Azure Cloud account and set up a new infrastructure
- Overview of the different tools and resources available for configuring an Azure Cloud infrastructure
- Walkthrough of the steps involved in setting up a basic Azure Cloud infrastructure, such as creating virtual machines and configuring storage accounts

3. **Managing Azure Cloud Infrastructure**

- Discussion of how to manage an existing Azure Cloud infrastructure, such as monitoring performance and scaling resources
- Overview of some of the different management tools available for Azure Cloud Infrastructure, such as Azure Portal and Azure PowerShell

- Explanation of how to automate common management tasks using tools like Azure Resource Manager and Azure Automation

4. **Securing Azure Cloud Infrastructure**

- Discussion of the different security risks associated with Azure Cloud Infrastructure, such as data breaches and malware attacks
- Overview of the different security features built into Azure Cloud Infrastructure, such as network security groups and encryption
- Explanation of best practices for securing an Azure Cloud infrastructure, such as setting up strong passwords and implementing multi-factor authentication

5. **Troubleshooting Azure Cloud Infrastructure**

- Explanation of some common issues that can arise when using Azure Cloud Infrastructure, such as connectivity problems and resource allocation errors
- Overview of the different troubleshooting tools and resources available for Azure Cloud Infrastructure, such as Azure Advisor and Azure Service Health
- Walkthrough of some common troubleshooting scenarios and how to resolve them using Azure Cloud Infrastructure tools and resources.

History

Azure Cloud is a cloud computing platform and service offered by Microsoft Corporation. The platform was announced in October 2008 under the name "Windows Azure" and was officially launched on February 1, 2010. Initially, Azure provided only platform-as-a-service (PaaS) and software-as-a-service (SaaS) offerings, but later Microsoft added infrastructure-as-a-service (IaaS) capabilities.

In the early days, Azure was primarily focused on providing a development and deployment platform for Windows-based applications. However, over time, Microsoft expanded the platform to support a wide range of operating systems, programming languages, and frameworks.

One of the significant milestones in the history of Azure was the release of Azure Virtual Machines in 2012, which allowed customers to run their own virtual machines in Azure's cloud infrastructure. This release marked a significant shift in Azure's strategy, as Microsoft recognized the growing demand for IaaS offerings.

In 2014, Microsoft rebranded Windows Azure as "Microsoft Azure," signaling a shift in the company's approach to the platform, emphasizing its multi-cloud and multi-operating system capabilities.

Since then, Microsoft has continued to expand Azure's capabilities, including adding support for Kubernetes, enabling customers to run containerized applications in Azure. They have also added a range of services, such as Azure Functions, Azure Cognitive Services, and Azure IoT Hub.

As of 2021, Azure is one of the leading cloud computing platforms, with a broad range of services and capabilities that enable organizations to build, deploy, and manage applications and services in the cloud.

CHAPTER I: INTRODUCTION TO AZURE CLOUD INFRASTRUCTURE

Azure Cloud Infrastructure is a collection of cloud-based services and resources provided by Microsoft's Azure platform that allows organizations to create and manage their own cloud-based environments. Azure Cloud Infrastructure provides various computing resources such as virtual machines, storage, networking, and database services that can be accessed remotely over the internet.

Azure Cloud Infrastructure is built on a global network of data centers that are geographically distributed to provide high availability and scalability. This means that an organization can create virtual machines and storage accounts in different regions around the world to provide low latency access for its users and customers.

Azure Cloud Infrastructure works by providing a range of services and tools that can be used to create and manage a cloud environment. The Azure Portal is the primary web-based interface for managing Azure Cloud Infrastructure, allowing users to create and manage resources such as virtual machines, storage accounts, and network configurations.

Azure Cloud Infrastructure also provides a number of APIs and command-line interfaces, such as Azure PowerShell and Azure CLI, which can be used to automate the creation and management of resources in the cloud. Azure Resource Manager (ARM) is a service that provides a way to manage resources in Azure Cloud Infrastructure as a single unit, rather than individually.

Azure Cloud Infrastructure is a comprehensive suite of cloud-based services that provides organizations with a wide range of computing, storage, and networking resources to create and manage their own cloud environments. Here is an overview of some of the different components of Azure Cloud Infrastructure:

1. **Virtual Machines**: Azure provides a wide range of virtual machine (VM) sizes and types that can be used to run different workloads, such as web applications, databases, and analytics tools. Azure virtual machines are based on different operating systems, including Windows and Linux, and can be configured with different amounts of memory, CPU, and storage resources.

2. **Storage Accounts**: Azure provides different types of storage accounts, including Blob storage, File storage, and Queue storage, that can be used to store and manage different types of data. Blob storage is used to store unstructured data, such as images, videos, and documents, while File storage provides a shared storage solution for multiple VMs. Queue storage is used to store messages that are processed asynchronously.

3. **Networks:** Azure provides a range of networking services, such as virtual networks (VNets), load balancers, and virtual private networks (VPNs), that can be used to connect different resources in the cloud. VNets allow organizations to create isolated network environments within Azure, while load balancers distribute traffic across different VMs to ensure high availability and scalability. VPNs allow organizations to securely connect their on-premises networks to Azure.

4. **Databases**: Azure provides a range of database services, such as SQL Database, Azure Cosmos DB, and Azure Database for PostgreSQL, that can be used to store and manage different types of data. SQL Database is a fully managed relational database service, while Azure Cosmos DB is a globally distributed NoSQL database service.

Azure Database for PostgreSQL is a managed PostgreSQL database service.

5. **Security**: Azure provides a range of security services and features to help organizations protect their data and resources in the cloud. These include Azure Security Center, which provides threat detection and response capabilities, and Azure Active Directory, which provides identity and access management services.

In summary, Azure Cloud Infrastructure provides a wide range of services and resources that organizations can use to create and manage their own cloud environments, including virtual machines, storage accounts, networks, databases, and security services.

There are many benefits of using Azure Cloud Infrastructure, which is why it has become such a popular choice for organizations of all sizes. Here are some of the key benefits:

1. **Scalability**: Azure Cloud Infrastructure is highly scalable, which means that organizations can easily add or remove resources as their needs change. This allows organizations to scale up or down quickly in response to changes in

demand or usage, without having to invest in new hardware or infrastructure.

2. **Flexibility**: Azure Cloud Infrastructure is flexible, which means that organizations can choose the resources they need to build the cloud environment that works best for their specific needs. This allows organizations to create custom environments that can be tailored to their specific requirements, without having to compromise on functionality or performance.

3. **Cost-Effective**: Azure Cloud Infrastructure is cost-effective, as it allows organizations to pay only for the resources they use. This eliminates the need for organizations to invest in costly hardware or infrastructure that may not be fully utilized, reducing overall costs and increasing efficiency.

4. **Reliability**: Azure Cloud Infrastructure is highly reliable, as it is built on a global network of data centers that are geographically distributed. This means that organizations can achieve high levels of uptime and availability for their applications and services, even in the event of a disaster or outage.

5. **Security**: Azure Cloud Infrastructure provides a wide range of security features and services that help organizations protect their data and resources in the cloud. These include

advanced threat detection and response capabilities, as well as identity and access management services.

6. Innovation: Azure Cloud Infrastructure is constantly evolving, with new services and features being added all the time. This allows organizations to take advantage of the latest technologies and innovations, without having to invest in costly hardware or infrastructure upgrades.

In summary, Azure Cloud Infrastructure provides many benefits to organizations, including scalability, flexibility, cost-effectiveness, reliability, security, and innovation. These benefits allow organizations to create and manage cloud environments that are tailored to their specific needs, while also achieving high levels of performance and efficiency.

QUESTIONS AND ANSWERS

Q: What is Azure Cloud Infrastructure? A: Azure Cloud Infrastructure is a suite of cloud-based services that provides organizations with computing, storage, and networking resources to create and manage their own cloud environments.

Q: What are some of the benefits of using Azure Cloud Infrastructure? A: Some of the benefits of using Azure Cloud Infrastructure include scalability, flexibility, cost-effectiveness, reliability, security, and innovation.

Q: What are some of the components of Azure Cloud Infrastructure? A: Some of the components of Azure Cloud Infrastructure include virtual machines, storage accounts, networks, databases, and security services.

Q: How does Azure Cloud Infrastructure provide scalability? A: Azure Cloud Infrastructure provides scalability by allowing organizations to easily add or remove resources as their needs change, without having to invest in new hardware or infrastructure.

Q: How does Azure Cloud Infrastructure provide flexibility? A: Azure Cloud Infrastructure provides flexibility by allowing organizations to choose the resources they need to build the cloud environment that works best for their specific needs.

Q: How does Azure Cloud Infrastructure provide cost-effectiveness? A: Azure Cloud Infrastructure provides cost-effectiveness by allowing organizations to pay only for the resources they use, eliminating the need for costly hardware or infrastructure investments.

Q: How does Azure Cloud Infrastructure provide reliability? A: Azure Cloud Infrastructure provides reliability by being built on a global network of data centers that are geographically distributed, ensuring high levels of uptime and availability.

Q: How does Azure Cloud Infrastructure provide security? A: Azure Cloud Infrastructure provides security through advanced threat detection and response capabilities, as well as identity and access management services.

Q: What types of organizations can benefit from using Azure Cloud Infrastructure? A: Organizations of all sizes and industries can benefit from using Azure Cloud Infrastructure, as it provides a wide range of services and resources that can be tailored to specific needs and requirements.

QUESTIONS

1. What is Azure Cloud Infrastructure?
2. What are some of the benefits of using Azure Cloud Infrastructure?
3. What are some of the key components of Azure Cloud Infrastructure?
4. How does Azure Cloud Infrastructure provide scalability?
5. How does Azure Cloud Infrastructure provide flexibility?
6. How does Azure Cloud Infrastructure provide cost-effectiveness?
7. How does Azure Cloud Infrastructure provide reliability?
8. How does Azure Cloud Infrastructure provide security?
9. What types of organizations can benefit from using Azure Cloud Infrastructure?
10. What are some examples of use cases for Azure Cloud Infrastructure?

CHAPTER II: SETTING UP AN AZURE CLOUD INFRASTRUCTURE

- Explanation of how to create an Azure Cloud account and set up a new infrastructure

To create an Azure Cloud account and set up a new infrastructure, follow these steps:

1. Go to the Azure website: Go to the Azure website at https://azure.microsoft.com/.

2. Sign up for an account: Click on the "Start free" button on the Azure homepage and follow the prompts to sign up for an Azure account. You will need to provide your personal information and payment details to complete the sign-up process.

3. Navigate to the Azure portal: Once you have signed up for an account, navigate to the Azure portal by clicking on the "Portal" button in the top right corner of the Azure homepage.

4. Create a new resource group: In the Azure portal, click on the "Resource groups" option in the left-hand menu and then click on the "Add" button to create a new resource group. Give your resource group a name and select a region.

5. Create a new virtual network: Click on the "Virtual networks" option in the left-hand menu and then click on the "Add" button to create a new virtual network. Give your virtual network a name and select the resource group you just created.

6. Create a new subnet: Within your virtual network, create a new subnet by clicking on the "Subnets" option and then clicking on the "Add" button. Give your subnet a name and specify the IP address range.

7. Create a new virtual machine: Click on the "Virtual machines" option in the left-hand menu and then click on the "Add" button to create a new virtual machine. Select the resource group and virtual network you just created and follow the prompts to specify the operating system, size, and other details.

8. Configure security: Once you have created your virtual machine, configure security by adding network security groups, firewalls, and other security measures as necessary.

9. Start your virtual machine: Once you have configured your virtual machine, start it up and begin using your new Azure Cloud infrastructure.

Overall, creating an Azure Cloud account and setting up a new infrastructure requires some technical expertise and knowledge of Azure's tools and services. However, with the right guidance and resources, anyone can create a new Azure infrastructure and take advantage of the benefits of cloud computing.

Azure Cloud Infrastructure offers a wide range of tools and resources that allow users to configure and manage their infrastructure efficiently. Here is an overview of some of the essential tools and resources available for configuring an Azure Cloud infrastructure:

1. Azure Portal: The Azure Portal is a web-based interface that provides a central location for managing Azure resources. The portal allows users to view and manage all Azure resources, such as virtual machines, storage accounts, and networks, in one place.

2. Azure CLI: Azure Command-Line Interface (CLI) is a command-line tool that allows users to manage Azure resources using a command-line interface. Azure CLI is available for Windows, macOS, and Linux.

3. Azure PowerShell: Azure PowerShell is a command-line tool that allows users to automate Azure management tasks using PowerShell scripts. PowerShell is a powerful scripting language that can be used to manage Azure resources.

4. Azure Resource Manager (ARM): Azure Resource Manager is a management framework that allows users to deploy and manage Azure resources in a consistent and repeatable way. ARM enables users to define and deploy complex infrastructure setups using templates.

5. Azure DevOps: Azure DevOps is a cloud-based platform for software development and delivery. DevOps includes tools for continuous integration and continuous delivery (CI/CD), automated testing, and project management.

6. Azure Advisor: Azure Advisor is a tool that provides personalized recommendations to optimize Azure resources' performance, security, and cost. It uses machine learning to analyze your Azure usage and provide recommendations for improving your infrastructure.

7. Azure Security Center: Azure Security Center is a tool that provides threat protection for your Azure resources. It provides security recommendations and alerts for potential security issues.

Overall, Azure Cloud Infrastructure offers a wide range of tools and resources that allow users to configure and manage their infrastructure effectively. These tools can help users optimize their infrastructure for performance, security, and cost-effectiveness.

basic walkthrough of the steps involved in setting up a basic Azure Cloud infrastructure, including creating virtual machines and configuring storage accounts:

1. Create an Azure account: Go to the Azure portal and sign up for an account. You can choose between a free or paid account, depending on your needs.
2. Create a resource group: A resource group is a logical container for Azure resources that share the same lifecycle. Go to the Azure portal and create a new resource group.
3. Create a virtual network: A virtual network allows you to create a private network within Azure that your virtual machines can connect to. Create a virtual network and subnets within it.
4. Create a storage account: A storage account is used to store data in Azure, such as virtual hard disks or data files. Create a storage account and configure its settings, such as replication options.
5. Create virtual machines: A virtual machine is a virtualized computer that can run an operating system and applications. Create virtual machines within your virtual network, specifying details such as the size, operating system, and storage options.

6. Configure networking: Connect your virtual machines to the virtual network you created earlier. You can also configure endpoints to allow traffic into your virtual machines from the internet or other networks.

7. Configure security: Azure provides various security features, such as firewalls and network security groups. Configure these to ensure that your infrastructure is secure.

8. Configure backups: Azure provides backup services that allow you to protect your data and virtual machines. Configure backups to ensure that your data is safe in the event of a disaster.

9. Monitor your infrastructure: Azure provides various monitoring tools that allow you to monitor the performance and health of your infrastructure. Configure monitoring to ensure that you can quickly detect and resolve issues.

This is just a basic walkthrough of setting up an Azure Cloud infrastructure. The specific steps and settings will vary depending on your needs and requirements.

Questions and answers

Q: What is a resource group in Azure? A: A resource group is a logical container for Azure resources that share the same lifecycle. Resources can be added, updated, or deleted together as a group.

Q: What is a virtual network in Azure? A: A virtual network allows you to create a private network within Azure that your virtual machines can connect to. This provides isolation and security for your infrastructure.

Q: What is a storage account in Azure? A: A storage account is used to store data in Azure, such as virtual hard disks or data files. It provides durable, highly available, and massively scalable storage.

Q: What is a virtual machine in Azure? A: A virtual machine is a virtualized computer that can run an operating system and applications. It allows you to run workloads in the cloud that require more resources than a traditional web or mobile app.

Q: What is a network security group in Azure? A: A network security group is a firewall that filters network traffic to and from Azure resources. It allows you to create security rules that determine which traffic is allowed and which is blocked.

Q: What is Azure Backup? A: Azure Backup is a service that allows you to protect your data and virtual machines by backing them up to Azure. It provides backup and restore capabilities for virtual machines, files, and folders.

Q: What is Azure Monitor? A: Azure Monitor is a service that allows you to monitor the performance and health of your Azure resources. It provides metrics, logs, and alerts that help you detect and diagnose issues in your infrastructure.

Q: What are the benefits of setting up an Azure Cloud infrastructure? A: Some of the benefits of setting up an Azure Cloud infrastructure include scalability, flexibility, high availability, security, and cost-effectiveness. It allows you to run workloads in the cloud that require more resources than a traditional web or mobile app, and it provides a wide range of tools and services to help you manage and monitor your infrastructure.

Questions

1. What is the purpose of a resource group in Azure?
2. What is a virtual network and why is it important in Azure?
3. What type of data can be stored in a storage account in Azure?
4. What is a virtual machine in Azure and what are its benefits?
5. How does a network security group work in Azure?
6. What is the purpose of Azure Backup?
7. What is Azure Monitor and how can it help with managing an Azure infrastructure?
8. What are some of the benefits of setting up an Azure Cloud infrastructure?

Key terms

1. Azure Cloud Infrastructure
2. Virtual Machine
3. Resource Group
4. Virtual Network
5. Storage Account
6. Network Security Group
7. Azure Backup
8. Azure Monitor
9. High Availability

10. Scalability

11. Flexibility

12. Cost-effectiveness

13. Azure Portal

14. Azure PowerShell

15. Azure Command-Line Interface (CLI)

CHAPTER III: MANAGING AZURE CLOUD INFRASTRUCTURE

Managing Azure cloud infrastructure requires a combination of technical skills, operational expertise, and understanding of best practices. Here are some key steps that can help you effectively manage your Azure infrastructure:

1. Plan and Design: Before deploying any resources on Azure, it is important to plan and design your infrastructure carefully. This involves defining your business requirements, identifying the Azure services you need, and designing a scalable and resilient architecture.

2. Deployment: Once you have a solid plan in place, you can deploy your infrastructure on Azure. You can use Azure

Resource Manager templates, PowerShell scripts, or Azure CLI to automate your deployment.

3. Monitoring: After deployment, it is important to monitor your Azure infrastructure to ensure that it is performing as expected. You can use Azure Monitor to collect data from various sources, including Azure services, third-party applications, and custom data sources.

4. Security: Azure offers a variety of security features to help you protect your infrastructure and data. This includes network security groups, virtual network firewalls, Azure Active Directory, and Azure Security Center.

5. Backup and Disaster Recovery: Azure provides built-in backup and disaster recovery solutions for your infrastructure. You can use Azure Backup to protect your data, and Azure Site Recovery to replicate and recover your applications and services.

6. Optimization: As your infrastructure grows, it is important to optimize your resources to ensure that you are getting the most value from your investment. You can use Azure Advisor and Azure Cost .

7. Management to identify opportunities to optimize your infrastructure.

8. Governance: To ensure that your infrastructure complies with regulatory and organizational policies, you can use

Azure Policy to enforce policies and Azure Governance to manage your subscriptions and resources.

By following these steps, you can effectively manage your Azure infrastructure and ensure that it is secure, scalable, and optimized for your business needs.

Managing an existing Azure Cloud infrastructure requires ongoing monitoring, optimization, and scaling to ensure that it meets the changing needs of your organization. Here are some key strategies for managing an existing Azure infrastructure:

1. Monitoring: Azure offers a variety of monitoring tools, including Azure Monitor, which can collect telemetry data from Azure services, third-party applications, and custom sources. You can use this data to track performance metrics, diagnose issues, and identify opportunities for optimization.

2. Optimization: As your infrastructure grows and changes, it is important to continuously optimize your resources to ensure that you are getting the most value from your investment. This includes identifying underutilized resources, optimizing resource configurations, and adjusting resource allocation as needed.

3. Scaling: Azure allows you to scale your resources up or down as needed to meet changing demand. This can be done manually or through automated scaling policies based on metrics such as CPU utilization or request rates.

4. Automation: Azure offers a variety of automation tools, including Azure Resource Manager templates, PowerShell scripts, and Azure CLI. These tools can be used to automate common tasks such as resource deployment, configuration management, and scaling.

5. Security: It is important to ensure that your Azure infrastructure is secure and meets regulatory compliance requirements. This includes implementing network security groups, virtual network firewalls, Azure Active Directory, and Azure Security Center.

6. Backup and Disaster Recovery: Azure provides built-in backup and disaster recovery solutions for your infrastructure. You can use Azure Backup to protect your data, and Azure Site Recovery to replicate and recover your applications and services in the event of an outage.

By following these strategies, you can effectively manage your existing Azure infrastructure, ensure that it is secure and optimized, and scale it as needed to meet the changing needs of your organization.

Managing Azure Cloud Infrastructure can be done through various tools and interfaces. Here are some of the different management tools available for Azure:

1. Azure Portal: A web-based interface for managing Azure resources and services. It provides a graphical user interface to manage Azure resources such as virtual machines, storage, and networking.

2. Azure PowerShell: A command-line interface for managing Azure resources using Windows PowerShell. It enables users to automate common tasks and manage resources from the command line.

3. Azure CLI: A cross-platform command-line interface for managing Azure resources. It supports multiple operating systems such as Windows, macOS, and Linux.

4. Azure Cloud Shell: An interactive, browser-accessible shell for managing Azure resources. It provides a command-line interface that can be used to manage Azure resources using Azure CLI or Azure PowerShell.

5. Azure Management APIs: A set of REST APIs for programmatically managing Azure resources. It enables developers to integrate Azure management capabilities into their own applications and services.

By leveraging these different tools and interfaces, users can manage their Azure resources more efficiently and effectively.

Automation of common management tasks in Azure Cloud Infrastructure can significantly reduce manual efforts and improve operational efficiency. Here are some tools available in Azure for automating common management tasks:

1. Azure Resource Manager: A service for managing Azure resources that enables users to create, update, and delete resources through a declarative JSON template. It simplifies management and deployment of Azure resources by grouping resources into a single unit, called a resource group.
2. Azure Automation: A cloud-based service for automating Azure management tasks. It provides tools for creating, scheduling, and managing runbooks, which are sets of

instructions for performing common management tasks such as scaling virtual machines or backing up data.

3. Azure Functions: A serverless compute service that enables users to run event-driven code in the cloud. It allows for the creation of small, single-purpose functions that can be used to automate common management tasks.

4. Azure Logic Apps: A cloud-based service that enables users to create workflows for automating common tasks across multiple systems and services. It provides connectors for integrating with various Azure services and other applications.

By leveraging these automation tools, users can reduce manual efforts and improve operational efficiency. They can also create consistent and repeatable processes, reducing the likelihood of errors and increasing reliability.

Questions and answers

Q: What is Azure Resource Manager?

A: Azure Resource Manager is a service for managing Azure resources that enables users to create, update, and delete resources through a declarative JSON template. It simplifies management and deployment of Azure resources by grouping resources into a single unit, called a resource group.

Q: What is Azure Automation?

A: Azure Automation is a cloud-based service for automating Azure management tasks. It provides tools for creating, scheduling, and managing runbooks, which are sets of instructions for performing common management tasks such as scaling virtual machines or backing up data.

Q: How can Azure Functions be used to manage Azure Cloud Infrastructure?

A: Azure Functions is a serverless compute service that enables users to run event-driven code in the cloud. It allows for the creation of small, single-purpose functions that can be used to automate common management tasks, such as scaling virtual machines or updating storage accounts.

Q: What are some benefits of automating management tasks in Azure Cloud Infrastructure?

A: By automating management tasks in Azure Cloud Infrastructure, users can reduce manual efforts and improve operational efficiency. They can also create consistent and repeatable processes, reducing the likelihood of errors and increasing reliability.

Q: What is Azure Logic Apps?

A: Azure Logic Apps is a cloud-based service that enables users to create workflows for automating common tasks across multiple systems and services. It provides connectors for integrating with various Azure services and other applications.

Questions

1. What are some common management tasks that can be automated in Azure Cloud Infrastructure?
2. What is Azure Portal and how can it be used for managing Azure resources?
3. What is Azure PowerShell and how can it be used for managing Azure resources?
4. How does Azure Resource Manager simplify management and deployment of Azure resources?

5. What is the difference between Azure Functions and Azure Logic Apps?

key terms on" Managing Azure Cloud Infrastructure

1. Azure Portal
2. Azure PowerShell
3. Azure Resource Manager
4. Azure Automation
5. Runbooks
6. Azure Functions
7. Serverless computing
8. Workflows
9. Connectors
10. Resource group.

CHAPTER 4 : SECURING AZURE CLOUD INFRASTRUCTURE

Azure Cloud Infrastructure is susceptible to various security risks that can compromise the security and integrity of data stored in the cloud. These risks include:

1. **Data breaches**: Hackers can gain unauthorized access to Azure resources, including virtual machines, storage accounts, and databases, and steal sensitive data.

2. **Malware attacks**: Malware can infect Azure virtual machines and steal or corrupt data, compromise system performance, and disrupt business operations.

3. **Denial of service (DoS) attacks**: Attackers can launch DoS attacks against Azure resources, causing them to become unavailable and disrupting business operations.

4. **Phishing attacks**: Attackers can use social engineering techniques to trick Azure users into divulging sensitive information, such as login credentials and financial data.

5. **Insider threats**: Employees with privileged access to Azure resources can misuse their access rights to steal or corrupt data or launch cyber attacks.

To mitigate these security risks, it is important to implement strong security measures such as identity and access management, network security, threat detection, and data protection. Azure provides a range of security tools and services to help customers protect their Azure resources from these and other security threats.

> Azure Cloud Infrastructure offers several security features to help protect data and resources stored in the cloud. Some of these features include:

1. **Network Security Groups (NSGs):** NSGs are used to control inbound and outbound traffic to Azure resources. NSGs can be used to create firewall rules to block or allow traffic based on the source and destination IP addresses, protocols, and ports.

2. **Azure Active Directory (Azure AD):** Azure AD is a cloud-based identity and access management solution that provides single sign-on (SSO) access to Azure resources. Azure AD allows users to sign in once to access multiple resources without having to enter credentials each time.

3. **Encryption**: Azure offers several encryption options, including encryption at rest and in transit. Encryption at rest encrypts data while it is stored in Azure storage

accounts or virtual machines. Encryption in transit encrypts data while it is being transmitted over the network.

4. **Azure Security Center**: Azure Security Center is a centralized security management solution that provides visibility into security threats and compliance issues across Azure resources. It provides recommendations for improving security posture and offers threat detection and response capabilities.

5. **Azure DDoS Protection**: Azure DDoS Protection is a service that protects against distributed denial of service (DDoS) attacks. It provides automatic detection and mitigation of DDoS attacks to ensure that Azure resources remain available to users.

Implementing these and other security features can help protect Azure resources from cyber attacks and other security threats.

Implementing strong passwords and multi-factor authentication are two important best practices for securing an Azure Cloud infrastructure. However, there are many other measures that can be taken to strengthen security. Here are some additional best practices to consider:

1. Regularly update and patch systems: Keeping software and systems up to date is critical for addressing vulnerabilities and reducing the risk of attacks.

2. Use network security groups (NSGs): NSGs can be used to restrict inbound and outbound traffic to Azure resources, providing an additional layer of protection.

3. Enable Azure Security Center: This service provides visibility into the security posture of an Azure environment and can alert administrators to potential security threats.

4. **Implement role-based access control (RBAC):** RBAC allows for the granting of granular permissions to users and groups, limiting the potential for unauthorized access.

5. Encrypt data at rest and in transit: Encryption helps to protect sensitive data from being accessed by unauthorized parties, both when it is stored and when it is transmitted.

6. Monitor logs and activity: Regularly reviewing logs and activity can help to detect anomalous behavior and identify potential security threats.

These are just a few examples of best practices for securing an Azure Cloud infrastructure. By implementing a comprehensive security strategy that includes these and other measures, organizations can help to protect their data and systems from potential cyber attacks.

CHAPTER 5: TROUBLESHOOTING AZURE CLOUD INFRASTRUCTURE

When using Azure Cloud Infrastructure, there are several common issues that users may encounter. These include:

1. **Connectivity problems**: Sometimes, users may experience issues connecting to their Azure resources or applications. This can be caused by a variety of factors, such as network latency, firewall issues, or misconfigured virtual networks.

2. **Resource allocation errors**: In some cases, users may receive error messages when attempting to allocate resources in Azure, such as virtual machines or storage accounts. This can occur when there is insufficient capacity in the user's subscription or when there are restrictions on the user's account.

3. **Performance issues**: Users may also experience performance issues when running applications or accessing

data in Azure. This can be caused by factors such as high network traffic or resource contention.

4. Security concerns: Users must ensure that their Azure Cloud Infrastructure is secure and protected from cyber threats. Failure to implement appropriate security measures can lead to data breaches or other security incidents.

5. Compliance requirements: Depending on the user's industry or location, there may be regulatory or compliance requirements that must be met when using Azure Cloud Infrastructure. Failure to comply with these requirements can result in legal or financial consequences.

To address these issues, users should consult Azure documentation and support resources, as well as regularly monitor their infrastructure for any potential issues or vulnerabilities. Implementing best practices for security, performance, and resource management can also help prevent common issues from arising.

Azure provides a range of tools and resources to help troubleshoot issues that may arise when using its cloud infrastructure. Some of these include:

1. **Azure Advisor**: This tool provides personalized recommendations to optimize Azure resources for cost, security, performance, and reliability.

2. Azure Service Health: This tool provides a personalized dashboard that displays the health of Azure services, including any ongoing incidents or planned maintenance.

3. Azure Monitor: This tool provides a centralized platform for monitoring Azure resources and applications, including performance metrics, logs, and alerts.

4. **Azure Network Watcher**: This tool provides a suite of network diagnostic and visualization tools, including packet capture, flow analysis, and connection troubleshooting.

5. Azure Resource Health: This tool provides real-time visibility into the health of individual Azure resources, including any issues or outages that may be impacting them.

By leveraging these tools, users can quickly identify and resolve any issues that may be impacting their Azure cloud infrastructure, helping to minimize downtime and optimize performance.

Common troubleshooting scenarios that can be resolved using Azure Cloud Infrastructure tools and resources:

1. Connectivity issues: If there are issues connecting to Azure resources, the Azure Network Watcher tool can be used to diagnose network connectivity problems and determine if any network security group rules are blocking traffic.

2. Resource allocation errors: If there are errors related to resource allocation, the Azure Advisor tool can be used to identify resource bottlenecks and provide recommendations for resource optimization.

3. Performance issues: If there are performance issues with Azure resources, the Azure Monitor tool can be used to monitor resource usage and identify performance bottlenecks.

4. **Service outages:** If there is a service outage, the Azure Service Health tool can be used to view the status of Azure services and receive notifications of service issues and planned maintenance.

5. Application errors: If there are application errors, the Azure Application Insights tool can be used to monitor application performance and identify errors and exceptions.

In each of these scenarios, the appropriate Azure Cloud Infrastructure tool or resource can be used to diagnose and resolve the issue.

Questions and Answers

1. What are some common issues that can arise when using Azure Cloud Infrastructure?

- Some common issues include connectivity problems, resource allocation errors, and issues with application performance.

2. What are some of the different troubleshooting tools available for Azure Cloud Infrastructure?

- Some tools include Azure Advisor, Azure Service Health, and Azure Monitor.

3. Can you give an example of a troubleshooting scenario and how it might be resolved using Azure Cloud Infrastructure tools?

- One example scenario could be a connectivity problem with a virtual machine. To troubleshoot this, you could use Azure Network Watcher to diagnose any network-related issues and check the status of network security groups. You could also use Azure Log Analytics to analyze log data and identify any potential issues with the VM's network configuration.

4. How can Azure Cloud Infrastructure be used to proactively monitor for potential issues?

- Azure Advisor can provide recommendations for optimizing and improving your infrastructure, while Azure Monitor can be used to monitor performance and receive alerts for potential issues.

5. What are some best practices for troubleshooting Azure Cloud Infrastructure issues?

- Some best practices include having a well-defined troubleshooting process, using appropriate tools and resources, and keeping up-to-date on the latest Azure Cloud Infrastructure updates and features. It is also important to document any issues and resolutions for future reference.

Azure glossary

1. Azure: A cloud computing platform and set of services provided by Microsoft.

2. Resource: An item within Azure that can be managed, such as a virtual machine or storage account.

3. Virtual machine: A software emulation of a computer system running within Azure.

4. Storage account: A place to store files and data within Azure.

5. Network: A collection of connected resources within Azure.

6. Load balancer: A service within Azure that distributes incoming traffic among multiple resources.

7. Availability set: A grouping of resources within Azure that ensures high availability by spreading them across multiple fault domains.

8. Region: A geographic location where Azure resources can be deployed and run.

9. Subscription: An agreement with Microsoft to use Azure services for a certain period of time.

10. Azure Active Directory: A cloud-based identity and access management service provided by Microsoft.

11. Azure Resource Manager: A service that helps users manage resources within Azure by grouping them together and applying policies and tags.

12. Azure Marketplace: An online store where users can browse and purchase third-party software and services to use within Azure.

13. Azure CLI: A command-line interface tool used to manage Azure resources and services.

14. Azure PowerShell: A PowerShell module used to manage Azure resources and services.

15. Azure DevOps: A suite of tools used for development, testing, and deployment of applications within Azure.

www.ingramcontent.com/pod-product-compliance
Lightning Source LLC
Chambersburg PA
CBHW070758220526
45467CB00014B/742